MW00852557

"In a modern world of electronic text excerpts and sound-bytes, Risa has gleaned pertinent questions from Jesus himself, and presented them for our real-time consideration. His questions are personal and subtly provoke us to entertain their relevance in life today. Enjoy this spiritual treat and savor its flavor."

SKIP FINCH, MISSION SEEKER AND HR PROFESSIONAL

"I absolutely love what you've written in the book. What a wonderful and tangible idea. I love the fact that the questions Jesus asked during His days on earth continue to speak to us today."

EVELYN CAPPER, FOLLOWER AND SCHOOL PRINCIPAL

"I can't wait to own a copy of this book. These are simple, everyday, common-sense truths that we, as Christians, conveniently—and continuously—forget. I know this: Were I to read this every day of the month it would be nothing short of life-changing."

BRIAN CASEY, ENTREPRENEUR AND CHURCH PLANTER

"I *love* this! I feel like your writing is an incredibly honest representation of the daily struggles of living a more Christ-like life. It can be extremely overwhelming to know where to start. I really love the personal touches. It makes it feel like I could just be sitting at your kitchen table (maybe a little coffee cake) having a conversation with you about God. Thank you so much for sharing."

JESSE MORENO, SEEKER AND BUSINESS PROFESSIONAL

"This is fabulous! Great study into the questions we need to ask ourselves and answer what God asks of us throughout the Bible."

STEPHANIE IDLAND, PERSON ON MISSION AND HR PROFESSIONAL

"It is thought-provoking and stabs one's mind with the reality that there's a Mighty God. It is a unique project designed for the awakening of God-consciousness to everyone whose path it will cross."

HENDRICKS OKEZIE, FOLLOWER AND BUSINESS OWNER

31 Questions Jesus Asked

QUESTIONS
JESUS
ASKED

RISA BAKER

PARTNERS 31, LLC
Atlanta

31 Questions Jesus Asked

These books are available at special discounts when purchased in quantity for use as premiums, promotions, fundraising, and group studies. For inquiries and details, contact the author at risa@risabaker.com

Published by Partners31, LLC
www.Partners31.com
Atlanta, Georgia

Cover & Interior Design by Imagine! Studios, LLC
www.ArtsImagine.com

Scripture quotations from THE MESSAGE. Copyright © by Eugene H. Peterson 1993, 1994, 1995, 1996, 2000, 2001, 2002. Used by permission of NavPress Publishing Group.

Scripture quotations marked (NLT) are taken from the Holy Bible, New Living Translation, copyright © 1996, 2004, 2007 by Tyndale House Foundation. Used by permission of Tyndale House Publishers, Inc., Carol Stream, Illinois 60188. All rights reserved.

Scripture quotations marked (ESV) are from The Holy Bible, English Standard Version® (ESV®), copyright © 2001 by Crossway, a publishing ministry of Good News Publishers. Used by permission. All rights reserved.

ISBN: 978-0-9895874-2-6
LCCN: 2013916733

First Partners31, LLC printing: November 2013

To my loving husband, Dan,
who inspires me to be a better person each day.

And to my children and grandchildren, all of whom I wish to
motivate and inspire to accept the legacy of Faith in Jesus.

CONTENTS

INTRODUCTION

God invited me on a journey when He gave me the assignment to write this book. Sitting in church one Sunday morning a few years ago, I listened to a sermon that came from Mark 4:35–41, the story where Jesus slept in the boat while a huge storm raged. His terrified disciples, certain they were about to die, woke Jesus and shouted, "Don't you care we are going to drown?" Jesus rebuked the winds and the waves, then turned and asked the disciples, "Why are you afraid? Do you still have no faith?"

Jesus' questions struck me. In fact, I heard very little of the rest of the sermon (Not to fault the preacher, my youngest brother!). The impact of the questions gripped me, and I knew I needed to have answers.

I have been a Christian since I was a young girl (A long time!). My husband and family are Christians, my parents are Christians, my grandparents were Christians, and my great-grandmother was a godly woman as well. My heritage of faith has been quite a blessing.

Despite that legacy, I felt fearful and less than faith-full many times. Hearing Jesus' questions that morning, I desired to have answers for Him. As Corrie ten Boom expressed, I longed to, "never be afraid to trust an unknown future to an all-knowing God!"

I began a study of the gospels (Matthew, Mark, Luke, and John). Along the way, I documented the questions Jesus asked—questions that deserved my answers. This incredible study gave me insights into my fears and my faith, and helped me to understand how vital it is to live in His forgiveness— both accepting it and extending it.

In Mark 4:2 we read, *"He taught by using stories, many stories"* (The Message). And in verses 4:33–34 we read, *"With many stories like these, he presented his message to them, fitting the stories to their experience and maturity. He was never without a story when he spoke. When he was alone with his disciples, he went over everything, sorting out the tangles, untying the knots"* (The Message).

God has impressed upon me to share with you the hope I discovered as He sorted out my "tangles and knots."

> *When life is heavy and hard to take,*
> *go off by yourself.*
> *Enter the silence. Bow in prayer.*
> *Don't ask questions:*
> ***Wait for hope to appear.***

LAMENTATIONS 3:28–29 (THE MESSAGE)

Hope. I don't know if you have a favorite word, but mine is hope. Hope makes my heart overflow.

Without hope, life seems overwhelming, defeating, and not worth living.

When our younger daughter, Mary, was 12, we lived in Austin, Texas, where she attended a fairly large public middle school. One afternoon, she came home and handed me a note. My heart broke as I read that a young lady had ended her life earlier that day by hanging herself in the school bathroom. I immediately wondered what would make the world seem so hopeless this girl was driven to end her short life.

Without hope life feels impossible. Let Jesus' questions fuel your desire to be a better person and make a positive difference in others' lives. Let His words fill you with hope.

Please read this book with a mind that is open to the words, thoughts, and answers that come to you. Write them down. The act of writing helps us to remember and encourages us to be open, honest, and vulnerable with ourselves and God. We must be all these things to experience lasting, positive change.

I hope you find Jesus' questions riveting, dynamic, thought-provoking, and most of all motivating, creating a readiness to change. Hope in God and share that hope with others!

Answering the **powerful questions Jesus asked** will give you strength. You will find the courage and faith that overcomes fear, and the freedom of living in daily forgiveness.

Anyone who wants to live all out for Christ is in for a lot of trouble; there's no getting around it . . . But don't let it faze you . . .

There's nothing like the written Word of God for showing you the way to salvation through faith in Christ Jesus.

Every part of Scripture is God-breathed and useful one way or another—showing us truth, exposing our rebellion, correcting our mistakes, training us to live God's way.

Through the Word we are put together and shaped up for the tasks God has for us.

II TIMOTHY 3:12–17 (THE MESSAGE)

Shape up for the tasks. **Answer what Jesus asked.**

My Prayer

*If I make you light-bearers, you don't think I'm
going to hide you under a bucket, do you?*

I'm putting you on a light stand.

Now that I've put you there on a hilltop, on a light stand—shine!

Keep open house; be generous with your lives.

*By opening up to others, you'll prompt people to open
up with God, this generous Father in heaven.*

Matthew 5:15–16 (The Message)

WHO DO YOU SAY I AM?

When Jesus came to the region of Caesarea Philippi, he asked his disciples, "Who do people say that the Son of Man is?"

"Well," they replied, "some say John the Baptist, some say Elijah, and others say Jeremiah or one of the other prophets."

*Then he asked them, "**But who do you say I am?**"*

Simon Peter answered, "You are the Messiah, the Son of the living God."

Jesus replied, "You are blessed, Simon son of John, because my Father in heaven has revealed this to you. You did not learn this from any human being.

MATTHEW 16:13–17 (NLT)

Who is Jesus to you?

If you ask this question of others, you may hear the same answers the disciples gave: a prophet, a teacher, a religious scholar, a good man.

What is your response to this question?

Your answer should make a profound difference in the way you live your life.

The difference between Jesus and history's other religious revolutionaries are the claims He made. Jesus never angled for political power. He didn't try to set up a religion with rules and regulations to follow. Instead, He made the startling claims that He was the Son of God, and that He had come to solve the problem of sin.

Jesus' message is called the gospel or "good news," because it's wonderful news to every imperfect person (know anyone?) who wants to know a perfect God.

C. S. Lewis wrote,

I am trying here to prevent anyone saying the really foolish thing that people often say about Him: I'm ready to accept Jesus as a great moral teacher, but I don't accept his claim to be God. That is the one thing we must not say. A man who was merely a man and said the sort of things Jesus said would not be a great moral teacher. He would either be a lunatic—on a level with the man who says he is a poached egg—or else he would be the Devil of Hell. You must make your choice. Either this man was, and is, the Son of God; or else a madman or something worse. You can shut Him up for a fool, you can spit at Him and kill Him as a demon; or you can fall at His feet and call Him Lord and God. But let us not come with any patronizing nonsense about His being a great human teacher. He has not left that open to us. He did not intend to.

MERE CHRISTIANITY

"Who do you say I am?" He asks.

Do you believe Jesus is the Messiah, the Son of the living God? How does this belief change you?

There was no identity crisis in the life of Jesus Christ. He knew who He was. He knew where He had come from, and why He was here. And He knew where He was going. And when you are that liberated, then you can serve.

HOWARD HENDRICKS

MY THOUGHTS TO GOD:

I know Jesus came as the Messiah and is the Son of the living God. Knowing this should make me excited to share with others what I know. Dear God: May I overcome my identity crisis and know who I am, where I came from and why I am here, and be liberated to serve with the confidence of where I am going in mind.

YOUR THOUGHTS TO GOD:

Jesus is the Son of God. He is our savior who died on the cross to save us from our sins & Hell. He is my comforter, my friend, my teacher & he loves me.

He is the one I talk to about life
issues. He shows me the way.

CAN ALL YOUR WORRIES ADD A SINGLE MOMENT TO YOUR LIFE?

"No one can serve two masters. For you will hate one and love the other; you will be devoted to one and despise the other. You cannot serve both God and money.

"That is why I tell you not to worry about everyday life—whether you have enough food and drink, or enough clothes to wear. Isn't life more than food, and your body more than clothing? Look at the birds. They don't plant or harvest or store food in barns, for your heavenly Father feeds them. And aren't you far more valuable to him than they are? **Can all your worries add a single moment to your life?**

"And why worry about your clothing? Look at the lilies of the field and how they grow. They don't work or make their clothing, yet Solomon in all his glory was not dressed as beautifully as they are. And if God cares so wonderfully for wildflowers that are here today and thrown into the fire tomorrow, he will certainly care for you. Why do you have so little faith?

"So don't worry about these things, saying, 'What will we eat? What will we drink? What will we wear?' These things

dominate the thoughts of unbelievers, but your heavenly Father already knows all your needs. Seek the Kingdom of God above all else, and live righteously, and he will give you everything you need.

"So don't worry about tomorrow, for tomorrow will bring its own worries. Today's trouble is enough for today."

MATTHEW 6:24–34 (NLT)

"Can all your worries add a single moment to your life?"

In my head, the answer to this question is a resounding "NO." But my heart doesn't always feel so confident. The fact is, I do worry. And my worry doesn't change one thing! According to Jesus, this worry is an evidence of my lack of faith.

My problem (and maybe yours as well) is that it's easy to be preoccupied with my getting and wanting control, while failing to remember God provides all and controls all. He doesn't need my help, but He does ask for my trust and obedience.

Here's another way to frame the worry question: Which statement causes you the most anxiety?

- *There is no God.*
- *There is no money in the bank.*

Too often we worry about missing out and not having things. We worry about stockpiling money, food, clothes— you name it. We forget that God provides and He cares for us.

All worries present a choice:

- ❖ Faith vs. Fear
- ❖ Light vs. Darkness
- ❖ God vs. Money

Do you have faith that God will provide everything you need?

What does worry add to your life?

How do you seek the Kingdom of God above all else?

MY THOUGHTS TO GOD:

Lord, You feed the birds, and You said I am more valuable than they. Please help me to steep my life in God-reality. May I decrease my fear and increase my faith because You already know my needs. My piece in the puzzle is to seek Your kingdom and live righteously above all else, knowing that You will give me everything I need. May I realize with all my worrying I cannot add a single moment to my life. Worry is a total waste of time and energy!

YOUR THOUGHTS TO GOD:

Forgive me for not having enough faith Lord + that you will provide + wasting my time with worry.

DIDN'T I TELL YOU THAT YOU WOULD SEE GOD'S GLORY IF YOU BELIEVE?

A man named Lazarus was sick. He lived in Bethany with his sisters, Mary and Martha. So the two sisters sent a message to Jesus telling him, "Lord, your dear friend is very sick."

But when Jesus heard about it he said, "Lazarus's sickness will not end in death. No, it happened for the glory of God so that the Son of God will receive glory from this."

So although Jesus loved Martha, Mary, and Lazarus, he stayed where he was for the next two days. Finally, he said to his disciples, "Let's go back to Judea." . . . Then he said, "Our friend Lazarus has fallen asleep, but now I will go and wake him up."

The disciples said, "Lord, if he is sleeping, he will soon get better!" They thought Jesus meant Lazarus was simply sleeping, but Jesus meant Lazarus had died.

So he told them plainly, "Lazarus is dead. And for your sakes, I'm glad I wasn't there, for now you will really believe. Come, let's go see him."

. . . When Martha got word that Jesus was coming, she went to meet him. But Mary stayed in the house. Martha said to Jesus, "Lord, if only you had been here, my brother would not have died. But even now I know that God will give you whatever you ask."

Jesus told her, "Your brother will rise again."

"Yes," Martha said, "he will rise when everyone else rises, at the last day."

Jesus told her, "I am the resurrection and the life. Anyone who believes in me will live, even after dying. Everyone who lives in me and believes in me will never ever die. Do you believe this, Martha?"

"Yes, Lord," she told him. "I have always believed you are the Messiah, the Son of God, the one who has come into the world from God."

Then she returned to Mary. She called Mary aside from the mourners and told her, "The Teacher is here and wants to see you." So Mary immediately went to him.

When Mary arrived and saw Jesus, she fell at his feet and said, "Lord, if only you had been here, my brother would not have died." . . .

"Where have you put him?" he asked them.

They told him, "Lord, come and see."

"Roll the stone aside," Jesus told them.

But Martha, the dead man's sister, protested, "Lord, he has been dead for four days. The smell will be terrible."

*Jesus responded, **"Didn't I tell you that you would see God's glory if you believe?"***

So they rolled the stone aside . . . Then Jesus looked up to heaven and said, "Father, thank you for hearing me. You always hear me, but I said it out loud for the sake of all these people standing here, so that they will believe you sent me."

Then Jesus shouted, "Lazarus, come out!" And the dead man came out, his hands and feet bound in grave clothes, his face wrapped in a head cloth.

Jesus told them, "Unwrap him and let him go!"

JOHN 11:1-44 (NLT)

I *love* this story. It always makes me smile because I relate on so many levels.

- ❖ Jesus states this sickness is not fatal, yet Lazarus dies. I consider a sickness that results in death as fatal— just my human reasoning, right?

- ❖ He loves Lazarus but He did not rush, He waited. Waiting gave Him the opportunity to reveal God's glory. Do you ever struggle with waiting? Perhaps the next time God is waiting I should consider it an opportunity for God's glory to be revealed!

- ❖ The disciples do not understand that Lazarus is dead, not just resting. They're so literal!

- ❖ Martha and Mary have faith. Martha even says, "If you had been here, my brother would not have died. I know that whatever you ask God, He will give you; I know that he will be raised up; All along I have believed that you are the Messiah, the Son of God."

It's so easy to relate to life in terms of human reasoning—"Lord, he has been dead for four days. The smell will be terrible." This is totally something I would think and say.

Jesus loved Martha. He looks her in the eye and reminds her, "Didn't I tell you that you would see God's glory if you believe?" The thought of her brother being raised from the dead never entered her mind. We have to believe to see the glory of God because we cannot imagine it.

Do you have faith to believe and focus to receive the glory of God?

MY THOUGHTS TO GOD:

Sometimes—maybe most of the time—I am clueless. I don't see when You are about to give me new grounds for believing. I lack focus. I operate in human reasoning. I think "if you had been here this would not have happened." I believe, but I overlook the fact that impossible situations are opportunities for You to show me your glory. And You remind me, "Didn't I tell you that you would see God's glory if you believe?" Thank you!

YOUR THOUGHTS TO GOD:

Thank you God. I want to believe even when I can't see the glory of God. Because Lord I understand I cant imagine it + I am not suppose to know everything God has planned. I also know your plan is the best plan for me.

CAN YOU PICK GRAPES FROM THORN BUSHES, OR FIGS FROM THISTLES?

"You can enter God's Kingdom only through the narrow gate. The highway to hell is broad, and its gate is wide for the many who choose that way. But the gateway to life is very narrow and the road is difficult, and only a few ever find it.

"Beware of false prophets who come disguised as harmless sheep but are really vicious wolves. You can identify them by their fruit, that is, by the way they act. **Can you pick grapes from thorn bushes, or figs from thistles?** A good tree produces good fruit, and a bad tree produces bad fruit. A good tree can't produce bad fruit, and a bad tree can't produce good fruit. So every tree that does not produce good fruit is chopped down and thrown into the fire. Yes, just as you can identify a tree by its fruit, so you can identify people by their actions.

"Not everyone who calls out to me, 'Lord! Lord!' will enter the Kingdom of Heaven. Only those who actually do the will of my Father in heaven will enter. On judgment day many will say to me, 'Lord! Lord! We prophesied in your name and cast out demons in your name and performed many miracles *in your name.' But I will reply, 'I never knew you. Get away from me, you who break God's laws.'*

"Anyone who listens to my teaching and follows it is wise, like a person who builds a house on solid rock. Though the rain comes in torrents and the floodwaters rise and the winds beat against that house, it won't collapse because it is built on bedrock. But anyone who hears my teaching and doesn't obey it is foolish, like a person who builds a house on sand. When the rains and floods come and the winds beat against that house, it will collapse with a mighty crash."

When Jesus had finished saying these things, the crowds were amazed at his teaching, for he taught with real authority— quite unlike their teachers of religious law.

MATTHEW 7:13–29 (NLT)

Look at the many comparisons in this teaching by Jesus. No wonder the crowds were amazed! What do we need to learn? We can identify a tree by its fruit. We can identify people by their actions. People identify us by our actions and our actions will be judged by God.

- ❖ Are we listeners or hearers?
- ❖ Followers or foolish?
- ❖ Bedrock or sand?
- ❖ Strong or destroyed?
- ❖ Grapes or thorns?
- ❖ Known or unknown?

At the end of our lives will we be able to say we did the will of our Father in heaven?

"Thy kingdom come, thy will be done, on earth (By me!) as it is in heaven." Familiar words from a familiar prayer. Are they only words, or a way of life?

MY THOUGHTS TO GOD:

Can you pick grapes from thorn bushes or figs from thistles? Of course, the answer is no. May my actions identify me as a fruitful tree. May I be wise and listen to Your teaching and follow it and seek each day to do Your will in my life as Your will is always done in heaven.

YOUR THOUGHTS TO GOD:

God I pray I will be a
listener, follower, bedrock,
strong, produce good fruit
+ follow your teaching.

DO YOU LOVE ME?

Later, Jesus appeared again to the disciples beside the Sea of Galilee. This is how it happened. Several of the disciples were there—Simon Peter, Thomas (nicknamed the Twin), Nathanael from Cana in Galilee, the sons of Zebedee, and two other disciples.

Simon Peter said, "I'm going fishing."

"We'll come, too," they all said. So they went out in the boat, but they caught nothing all night.

At dawn Jesus was standing on the beach, but the disciples couldn't see who he was.

He called out, "Fellows, have you caught any fish?"

"No," they replied.

Then he said, "Throw out your net on the right-hand side of the boat, and you'll get some!" So they did, and they couldn't haul in the net because there were so many fish in it.

Then the disciple Jesus loved said to Peter, "It's the Lord!"

When Simon Peter heard that it was the Lord, he put on his tunic (for he had stripped for work), jumped into the water, and headed to shore. The others stayed with the boat and pulled the loaded net to the shore, for they were only about a hundred yards from shore. When they got there, they found breakfast waiting for them—fish cooking over a charcoal fire, and some bread.

"Bring some of the fish you've just caught," Jesus said. So Simon Peter went aboard and dragged the net to the shore. There were 153 large fish, and yet the net hadn't torn.

"Now come and have some breakfast!" Jesus said. None of the disciples dared to ask him, "Who are you?" They knew it was the Lord. Then Jesus served them the bread and the fish.

*After breakfast Jesus asked Simon Peter, "Simon son of John, **do you love me more than these?**"*

"Yes, Lord," Peter replied, "you know I love you."

"Then feed my lambs," Jesus told him.

*Jesus repeated the question: "Simon son of John, **do you love me?**"*

"Yes, Lord," Peter said, "you know I love you."

"Then take care of my sheep," Jesus said.

*A third time he asked him, "Simon son of John, **do you love me?**"*

Peter was hurt that Jesus asked the question a third time. He said, "Lord, you know everything. You know that I love you."

Jesus said, "Then feed my sheep.

JOHN 21: 1–17 (NLT)

Peter had been so confident in himself just a short time before Jesus was crucified. At their last supper he had said "I'll lay down my life for you!" (John 13:37, The Message) Jesus responded, "Really? You'll lay down your life for me? The truth is that before the rooster crows, you'll deny me three times." (John 13:38, The Message) How often are we so certain we will *never* do something and then we do it?

- I won't cheat on my spouse.
- I won't lie.
- I will give.
- I will trust and not interfere.

Three times Peter denied knowing Jesus. On the beach that morning, Peter affirmed his love for Jesus three times. The third time he admitted, "Master you know everything there is to know. You've got to know that I love you."

Even when I don't know myself, Jesus knows me. The same is true for you. When have you heard God's voice asking "Do you love me?"

Peter's denials were obviously something he never thought he would do.

What have you done you were certain you never would?

Completely forgiving Peter of his betrayal, Jesus moves forward and commands, "Follow me."

Do you think Peter was ready to follow? Did he understand that it would cost him his life? He was lovingly willing to do so, are you?

Jesus asked Peter to feed His sheep, lead His sheep and follow Him. Peter's answer—with his words and actions—was *yes*.

What have you been asked to do? Did you answer yes?

MY THOUGHTS TO GOD:

This is a simple question with a seemingly simple answer: Yes! But do my actions confirm my words? You know the dangers, deceitfulness, doubts far more than I do. May I find strength in you in my weakness and know that I clearly do not know what capabilities (both good and bad) I have. May I believe like Peter. Master you know everything there is to know! You've got to know that I love You. Help me to trust when You ask me to follow. I need the reminder!

YOUR THOUGHTS TO GOD:

I love you Lord, Thank you for loving me. Forgive me where I have failed you + show me the way you would have me go.

DO YOU WANT TO GET WELL?

Some time later, Jesus went up to Jerusalem for one of the Jewish festivals. Now there is in Jerusalem near the Sheep Gate a pool, which in Aramaic is called Bethesda and which is surrounded by five covered colonnades.

Here a great number of disabled people used to lie—the blind, the lame, the paralyzed. One who was there had been an invalid for thirty-eight years. When Jesus saw him lying there and learned that he had been in this condition for a long time, he asked him, **"Do you want to get well?"**

"Sir," the invalid replied, "I have no one to help me into the pool when the water is stirred. While I am trying to get in, someone else goes down ahead of me."

Then Jesus said to him, "Get up! Pick up your mat and walk." At once the man was cured; he picked up his mat and walked.

JOHN 5:1–9 (THE MESSAGE)

This man had been an invalid for thirty-eight years! Each day he hoped to find healing in the water but had no one to help him. Jesus simply asks, "Do you want to get well?"

The invalid man doesn't answer yes. He replies, "I have no one to help me." When Jesus commands, "Get up!" He is in effect saying, *I am here to help you. Will you let me?*

This man responded to Jesus' command and in an instant, his disability disappeared.

Jesus asks the same question of you. Do you want to get well? Jesus knows just how long you have been ill, physically, emotionally, and spiritually. He is the One who can help and heal you. Will you let Him?

MY THOUGHTS TO GOD:

Am I willing to let You make me well? Do I trust in faith that You know best for me? Of all the people at the pool that day, You chose this man to heal. What was it about him? Was it the length of time he had been ill, was it his helplessness, was it his desire to get well? May I not hinder Your work in my life by *not* believing You can make me well.

YOUR THOUGHTS TO GOD:

Lord make me well physically,
mental, emotionally + spiritually.
I want to be healed Lord.

7

ARE YOU ALSO GOING TO LEAVE?

"I tell you the truth, anyone who believes has eternal life. Yes, I am the bread of life! Your ancestors ate manna in the wilderness, but they all died. Anyone who eats the bread from heaven, however, will never die. I am the living bread that came down from heaven. Anyone who eats this bread will live forever; and this bread, which I will offer so the world may live, is my flesh."

Then the people began arguing with each other about what he meant. "How can this man give us his flesh to eat?" they asked.

He said these things while he was teaching in the synagogue in Capernaum.

Many of his disciples said, "This is very hard to understand. How can anyone accept it?"

Jesus was aware that his disciples were complaining, so he said to them, "Does this offend you? ...The Spirit alone gives eternal life. Human effort accomplishes nothing. And the very words I have spoken to you are spirit and life.

But some of you do not believe me." (For Jesus knew from the beginning which ones didn't believe, and he knew who would betray him.) Then he said, "That is why I said that people can't come to me unless the Father gives them to me."

At this point many of his disciples turned away and deserted him. Then Jesus turned to the Twelve and asked, "Are you also going to leave?"

Simon Peter replied, "Lord, to whom would we go? You have the words that give eternal life. We believe, and we know you are the Holy One of God."

Then Jesus said, "I chose the twelve of you, but one is a devil." He was speaking of Judas, son of Simon Iscariot, one of the Twelve, who would later betray him.

JOHN 6: 47–52; 59–71 (NLT)

Jesus knows when we have a hard time understanding. In this passage, His message was clear, yet difficult to comprehend—and perhaps even harder to believe. But Jesus didn't soften His message to make it easier to accept. Neither did He force people to accept Him. He always offers a choice. After all, He is a *gift* from the Father.

I love Peter's response when Jesus asked the Twelve if they wanted to leave. "Master to whom would we go?" Peter was committed and confident that Jesus was the Holy One of God.

When things are tough, do you want to leave? When there is something you don't like, don't agree with, can't justify, don't understand—do you want to leave?

Even one of the Twelve left.

Do you believe Jesus has the words of real life, eternal life? Are you confident He is the Holy One of God?

MY THOUGHTS TO GOD:

Lord, I am hand-picked by You—committed and confident You are the Holy One of God. I do *not* want to be the betrayer. Even when Your teachings are tough to swallow, may I have the grace and strength to learn, grow, and move forward—not give up and desert You. May I desire above all else to be associated with You.

Please help me to remember that You love me and You have the words of real life! Keep before me that *human effort accomplishes nothing.* We get to you only as a gift from the Father. Thank you, dear God, for that gift to me!

YOUR THOUGHTS TO GOD:

Lord I know you love me + you know what is best for me. Lord I want to accept what you have for me. I pray I will have the grace + strength to learn, grow + move forw and with you. Thank you Lord

_____

_____

_____

DON'T YOU REALIZE THAT I COULD ASK MY FATHER FOR THOUSANDS OF ANGELS TO PROTECT US, AND HE WOULD SEND THEM INSTANTLY?

So Judas came straight to Jesus. "Greetings, Rabbi!" he exclaimed and gave him the kiss.

Jesus said, "My friend, go ahead and do what you have come for."

Then the others grabbed Jesus and arrested him. But one of the men with Jesus pulled out his sword and struck the high priest's slave, slashing off his ear.

*"Put away your sword," Jesus told him. "Those who use the sword will die by the sword. **Don't you realize that I could ask my Father for thousands of angels to protect us, and he would send them instantly?** But if I did, how would the Scriptures be fulfilled that describe what must happen now?"*

Then Jesus said to the crowd, "Am I some dangerous revolutionary, that you come with swords and clubs to arrest me? Why didn't you arrest me in the Temple? I was there teaching every day. But this is all happening to fulfill the words of the prophets as recorded in the Scriptures." At that point, all the disciples deserted him and fled.

MATT. 26:49–56 (NLT)

Focused on completing His mission, Jesus felt no fear for his own protection. He knew the impending suffering and ultimate sacrifice of His life had to happen to fulfill the words of the prophets.

Although protection was available and within His power to command, Jesus knew escape was not the Father's will. Have you ever wondered why protection didn't come? Why would God deny His only son protection from this crowd and the horrors that would follow?

Those events—including the moment of self-sacrifice when Jesus allowed himself to be arrested—were all part of the Father's perfect plan. ***"Don't you realize that I could ask my Father for thousands of angels to protect us, and he would send them instantly?"*** Jesus, always in charge, willingly gave up his life to fulfill the Scriptures and provide the gift of salvation for us.

Hatred and fear drove the people in the garden that night.

The high priests and religious leaders came to the garden waving swords and clubs. Hatred consumed them. Jesus's teachings threatened their power. They wanted Him stopped. They wanted Him killed.

Fear squashed the faith of the disciples and they deserted Him and fled. Even after Jesus reassured them of His ultimate authority, they could only see that there would be no miracle this time. So they ran.

When faced with a crisis, will faith squash your fear or will fear lead to desertion?

MY THOUGHTS TO GOD:

I am certain I would've deserted You that night. May I always know that You have the power to protect me instantly, but it may not be Your will in every circumstance. May I have Your strength and wisdom to be certain of my mission and task and to be focused on fulfilling Your will rather than my protection. May my faith be strong enough to squash the fear.

YOUR THOUGHTS TO GOD:

Lord help me to except your will for me even if I don't understand it. Give me strength + wisdom to fulfill your will not mine. May my faith be strong.

Do you believe in the Son of Man?

John 9 tells the story of a man born blind and how he was healed inwardly and outwardly.

Walking down the street, Jesus saw a man blind from birth. His disciples asked, "Rabbi, who sinned: this man or his parents, causing him to be born blind?"

Jesus said, "You're asking the wrong question. You're looking for someone to blame. There is no such cause-effect here. Look instead for what God can do. We need to be energetically at work for the One who sent me here, working while the sun shines. When night falls, the workday is over. For as long as I am in the world, there is plenty of light. I am the world's light."

He said this and then spit in the dust, made a clay paste with the saliva, rubbed the paste on the blind man's eyes, and said, "Go, wash at the Pool of Siloam" (Siloam means "Sent"). The man went and washed—and saw.

Soon the town was buzzing . . . They said, "How did your eyes get opened? . . . They marched the man to the Pharisees . . . They said, "What did he do to you? How did he open your eyes?"

"I've told you over and over and you haven't listened. Why do you want to hear it again? Are you so eager to become his disciples? . . . They said, "You're nothing but dirt! How dare you take that tone with us!" Then they threw him out in the street.

Jesus heard that they had thrown him out, and went and found him. He asked him, "Do you believe in the Son of Man?"

The man said, "Point him out to me sir, so that I can believe in him.

Jesus said "You're looking right at him. Don't you recognize my voice?"

"Master, I believe," the man said and worshipped him.

John 9:1–8: 27–38 (The Message)

This man had been born blind, and on this day he was healed. He saw light for the first time. What should have been a great day of rejoicing quickly turned into a day of being harassed and ostracized! He surely must have felt confused and alone.

The religious leaders were not happy for him at all and threw him out into the street. That's where Jesus found him.

"Do you believe in the Son of Man?" He asked.

"I want to believe but I don't know who he is."

"You're looking right at him. *Don't you recognize my voice?*"

The blind man hadn't been able to see Jesus when He told him, "go wash in the Pool of Siloam." After the commotion and stress of the day, he didn't recognize Jesus's voice.

But when the man spoke with Jesus in the street, he finally recognized Him as the Son of Man. For a second time that day, the man's eyes were opened. He believed in and worshiped Jesus. In an instant, faith eliminated all his fear and confusion.

MY THOUGHTS TO GOD:

When my belief falters, I do not recognize your voice. Fear, confusion, stress, trying to do things my own way all cause doubt and lack of belief in You, the Son of Man. I ask the wrong questions, look for someone to blame, and shut out the light. UGH!!

Even worse, do I rejoice in others' healing or throw them out in the street?

I pray I would not have eyes that see yet are blind and unbelieving. May I look right at You and recognize Your voice and worship You, Jesus.

Your thoughts to God:

Open my eyes + ears to
you Lord

DON'T YOU UNDERSTAND YET?

Then the disciples came to him and asked, "Do you realize you offended the Pharisees by what you just said?"

Jesus replied, "Every plant not planted by my heavenly Father will be uprooted, so ignore them. They are blind guides leading the blind, and if one blind person guides another, they will both fall into a ditch."

Then Peter said to Jesus, "Explain to us the parable that says people aren't defiled by what they eat."

"Don't you understand yet?" Jesus asked. "Anything you eat passes through the stomach and then goes into the sewer. But the words you speak come from the heart—that's what defiles you. For from the heart come evil thoughts, murder, adultery, all sexual immorality, theft, lying, and slander. These are what defile you. Eating with unwashed hands will never defile you."

MATTHEW 15: 12–20 (NLT)

Don't you understand yet? God has spoken these words to me so many times. He reminds me again and again that following all the rules and appearing perfect doesn't equate to righteousness. It's the heart that counts.

"But the words you speak come from the heart—that's what defiles you." Thoughts and words turn into actions and behavior. If we want to be more like Him, we have to purify ourselves from the inside out—not the other way around.

In her book and devotional journal, *The Overflow of the Heart*, Carolyn Joy writes, "So how can you tell what is in your heart? . . . The answer is quite simple . . . the answer is pressure. The heart is a tube, and when pressure is applied, what comes out in words and actions is what is inside."

What comes out when your heart is "squeezed"? Evil thoughts, murder, adultery, immorality, theft, lying, and slander, or love, joy, peace, kindness, patience, and forgiveness?

It isn't our external appearance but our heart-driven thoughts, behaviors, and actions that reflect our purity. When under pressure and "squeezed," what comes from your heart? Are we blind guides leading the blind into a ditch? Do we understand what really matters to God?

MY THOUGHTS TO GOD:

I have so much to learn and understand! May I not be a blind guide. I want to be a light in darkness. My thoughts and words come from my heart, either defiled or pure and clean. May I always be open to Your radical teaching and in the pressures of life please help me to have understanding and give my heart to You. My prayer:

> *I will give them hearts that recognize me as the Lord. They will be my people, and I will be their God, for they will return to me wholeheartedly.*

JEREMIAH 24:7 (NLT)

YOUR THOUGHTS TO GOD:

Help me o Lord to have a kind
heart + speak encouragement,
uplifting, louing + kind words
out of my mouth to glorify
you O' Lord

But how much of that kind of persistent faith will the Son of Man find on the earth when he returns?

Jesus told them a story showing that it was necessary for them to pray consistently and never quit. He said, "There was once a judge in some city who never gave God a thought and cared nothing for people. A widow in that city kept after him: 'My rights are being violated. Protect me!'

"He never gave her the time of day. But after this went on and on he said to himself, 'I care nothing what God thinks, even less what people think. But because this widow won't quit badgering me, I'd better do something and see that she gets justice—otherwise I'm going to end up beaten black-and-blue by her pounding.'"

Then the Master said, "Do you hear what that judge, corrupt as he is, is saying? So what makes you think God won't step in and work justice for his chosen people, who continue to cry out for help? Won't he stick up for them? I assure you, he will. He will not drag his feet. **But how much of that kind of persistent faith will the Son of Man find on the earth when he returns?**"

Luke 18:1–8 (The Message)

D o I have persistent faith, or do I just give up? Even corrupt "judges" can be worn down when the cause is just and the petitioner is relentless. Won't God stick up for you and me? The key is praying consistently and not quitting. Hmm, I may need a little work on that one.

Prayer is powerful. Jesus spent hours in prayer. He taught the disciples to pray. If prayer was that important to him, shouldn't it be important to me?

Have you ever prayed for someone or something and then quit when God didn't immediately respond? We all have! But in this passage, Jesus tells us to have persistent faith—to pray without ceasing.

We read in the book, *The Help*, that Aibileen Clark wrote her prayers. Do you see a benefit to tracking your requests and God's responses? If you don't already, I'd like to challenge you to start keeping a journal of prayers and answers to those prayers. Doing so may help you be more consistent and persistent in your requests—and more mindful of the power of prayer. When you feel discouraged, go back and read your prayer journal and see how God has answered your prayers. Doing so will increase your faith.

MY THOUGHTS TO GOD:

I need prayer to have persistent faith. If it was important to You it *must* be important to me. Remembering how You have answered my prayers increases my faith and helps me not forget how wonderful, powerful, and faithful You are to me. As Your child, I know You only do what is best for me

and You tell me to ask for the desires of my heart. I want You
to find persistent faith in me.

YOUR THOUGHTS TO GOD:

Lord I want to have
more persistent faith I
trust that you will
answer my prayers.
I pray for the desires of
my heart. Amen.

Shouldn't You Have Mercy on Your Fellow Servant Just as I Had Mercy on You?

"Therefore, the Kingdom of Heaven can be compared to a king who decided to bring his accounts up to date with servants who had borrowed money from him. In the process, one of his debtors was brought in who owed him millions of dollars. He couldn't pay, so his master ordered that he be sold—along with his wife, his children, and everything he owned—to pay the debt.

"But the man fell down before his master and begged him, 'Please, be patient with me, and I will pay it all.' Then his master was filled with pity for him, and he released him and forgave his debt.

"But when the man left the king, he went to a fellow servant who owed him a few thousand dollars. He grabbed him by the throat and demanded instant payment.

"His fellow servant fell down before him and begged for a little more time. 'Be patient with me, and I will pay it,' he pleaded. But his creditor wouldn't wait. He had the man arrested and put in prison until the debt could be paid in full.

*"When some of the other servants saw this, they were very upset. They went to the king and told him everything that had happened. Then the king called in the man he had forgiven and said, 'You evil servant! I forgave you that tremendous debt because you pleaded with me. **Shouldn't you have mercy on your fellow servant, just as I had mercy on you?**' Then the angry king sent the man to prison to be tortured until he had paid his entire debt.*

"That's what my heavenly Father will do to you if you refuse to forgive your brothers and sisters from your heart."

MATTHEW 18:23–35 (NLT)

Every time I read this story my heart screams *that is so not right!* The unforgiving servant is so wrong, unfair, and ungrateful! At the same time, this riveting parable reminds me just how tough it is *not* to be the evil servant.

Logically we know that the answer to the king's question must be a resounding *"Yes!"* But it is far easier to talk about forgiveness than to actually forgive on a daily basis.

Is there someone you refuse to forgive? If someone has wronged or hurt you in some way, do you have the right to withhold forgiveness? If your instinct is to demand justice, consider this: Our tremendous debt has been forgiven. Shouldn't we be forgiving because we have been forgiven?

MY THOUGHTS TO GOD:

I have no right to be unforgiving, but You know I am *not* always forgiving. Change my heart so that I constantly remember You have forgiven *my* tremendous debt. Help me not to focus on trying to force someone else to pay. If I am truly thankful for the undeserved forgiveness You have given me, the least I can do is to forgive others who are undeserving.

YOUR THOUGHTS TO GOD:

Thank you Lord for
forgiving me + help me
to always be forgiving
of others

IF YOU DON'T FORGIVE SINS, WHAT ARE YOU GOING TO DO WITH THEM?

Later on that day, the disciples had gathered together, but, fearful of the Jews, had locked all the doors in the house. Jesus entered, stood among them, and said, "Peace to you." Then he showed them his hands and side.

The disciples, seeing the Master with their own eyes, were exuberant. Jesus repeated his greeting: "Peace to you. Just as the Father sent me, I send you."

*Then he took a deep breath and breathed into them. "Receive the Holy Spirit," he said. "If you forgive someone's sins, they're gone for good. **If you don't forgive sins, what are you going to do with them?**"*

JOHN 20:19–23 (THE MESSAGE)

I t was resurrection day and Jesus had already visited several of his followers. Lacking faith, the disciples hid in fear together behind locked doors. When Jesus entered the house and said, "Peace to you," the mood shifted dramatically. They became overjoyed, *exuberant*. Then Christ reaffirmed their purpose: "Just as the Father sent me, so I send you." He then took a deep breath and breathed into them the Holy Spirit. With the next breath He spoke about forgiveness. Does this seem odd to you? Why not give them marching orders or an explanation for his sudden presence? Instead, He made a profound statement and asked an equally profound question: "If you forgive someone's sins, they're gone for good . . . ***If you don't forgive sins, what are you going to do with them?***"

How would you answer that question? I didn't have an answer! It forced me to stop and think. Finally, I came to the conclusion that the only way to do away with sin for good, is to forgive it! Isn't that exactly what Jesus does for us?

If we don't forgive sins we become angry, bitter, distrustful, judgmental, and the nail in the coffin: *unloving*. Love is supposed to be our trademark!

> *Your love for one another will prove to the world that you are my disciples."*
>
> JOHN 13:35 (NLT)

As human beings, the only possible way to live in forgiveness is through the Holy Spirit. If the disciples chose to hold onto a spirit of anger and bitterness rather than being filled with the Holy Spirit and forgive and love people, how far would they have gotten in their mission to share the Good News?

What about you? What are you doing with the wrongs you've committed as well as those committed against you? Are you holding onto feelings of judgment and distrust? Does lack of forgiveness keep you from loving God's way?

I believe that a lack of love toward others does more to harm the Kingdom cause than anything else. Whatever hurts you're holding onto, choose to let go and forgive. Choose to love. After all, that's what Jesus did for you and me.

MY THOUGHTS TO GOD:

You convict my heart, Lord. I know that being unwilling to forgive makes me unloving and unrecognizable as Your disciple. Please keep this question before me: *If you don't forgive sins, what are you going to do with them?* I need to remember I willingly accept Your gift of forgiveness to me. I don't want to be unwilling to share that same gift with others. I don't want to be the unforgiving servant! (Matthew 18:21–35) I have always hated that injustice. How could I not be willing to extend to others the kindness and forgiveness You've shown me?

YOUR THOUGHTS TO GOD:

_____

_____

_____

_____

YOU PARENTS—IF YOUR CHILDREN ASK FOR A LOAF OF BREAD, DO YOU GIVE THEM A STONE INSTEAD?

"Keep on asking, and you will receive what you ask for. Keep on seeking, and you will find. Keep on knocking, and the door will be opened to you. For everyone who asks, receives. Everyone who seeks, finds; and to everyone who knocks, the door will be opened.

"You parents—if your children ask for a loaf of bread, do you give them a stone instead? *Or if they ask for a fish, do you give them a snake? Of course not! So if you sinful people know how to give good gifts to your children, how much more will your heavenly Father give good gifts to those who ask him."*

MATTHEW 7:7–11 (NLT)

I have been a parent for more than thirty years. Not once have I ever intentionally *not* had my children's best interests at heart. Have I made mistakes? You bet! (Just ask my children—I am sure they would be happy to share.) But my desire has always been to bless and help them.

If my children asked for food, of course they got food—not a stone or a snake. I love them and enjoy giving them good gifts. But as much as I care for them, I can in *no way* compare to how much our heavenly Father loves us and wants to give us good gifts!

But we must follow His instructions! (Have you ever tried to put something together without following the instructions?)

Keep on asking and we will receive.

Keep on seeking and we will find.

Keep on knocking and the door will be opened.

Don't give up.

Do you believe the heavenly Father loves you and wants to give you good gifts? What are some specific gifts you have received?

My thoughts to God:

Father, as a parent I understand Your point. If I, a sinful parent, give good gifts to my children, how much more will You bless me? Increase my faith so that I will keep on asking, seeking, and knocking. May I remember all the good gifts You have given already and know that You always will do what is best for me.

YOUR THOUGHTS TO GOD:

_____

_____

_____

_____

_____

_____

_____

_____

_____

_____

Is anything worth more than your soul?

From then on Jesus began to tell his disciples plainly that it was necessary for him to go to Jerusalem, and that he would suffer many terrible things at the hands of the elders, the leading priests, and the teachers of religious law. He would be killed, but on the third day he would be raised from the dead.

But Peter took him aside and began to reprimand him for saying such things. "Heaven forbid, Lord," he said. "This will never happen to you!"

Jesus turned to Peter and said, "Get away from me, Satan! You are a dangerous trap to me. You are seeing things merely from a human point of view, not from God's."

Then Jesus said to his disciples, "If any of you wants to be my follower, you must turn from your selfish ways, take up your cross, and follow me. If you try to hang on to your life, you will lose it. But if you give up your life for my sake, you will save it. **And what do you benefit if you gain the whole world but lose your own soul? Is anything worth more than your soul?** For the Son of Man will come with *his angels in the glory of his Father and will judge all people according to their deeds.*

MATTHEW 16:21–27 (NLT)

"Is anything worth more than your soul?" I intellectually know that the answer to this question is: "No, *nothing* is worth more than my soul." But, honestly, I don't always live that way. At times, I have been like Peter, a dangerous trap. Too often, I see things from my human point of view, rather than from God's perspective.

Peter did not like what Jesus had to say. His Master was going to Jerusalem to suffer and die at the hands of the "religious" leaders. It didn't make sense! I wouldn't be surprised if Peter momentarily tuned out after Jesus said He was going to be killed. Did Peter even hear his Lord say He would be raised from the dead? Or did he focus so intently on the bad news that he missed the good news?

After Jesus calls Peter out, He offers some much-needed perspective. The New Living Translation of Matthew 16:25 reads:

If you try to hang on to your life, you will lose it. But if you give up your life for my sake, you will save it.

In other words, if you want to micro-manage life toward safety and comfort, you'll end up losing your soul. If you want to *really* live, turn from selfish ways, take up your cross and follow Jesus. You'll be amazed at the joy and freedom you'll find.

Give up your life for His sake and He will save you. Is your soul worth that?

How can we see things from God's view rather than our human point of view?

Do you think this is a matter of *faith?*

MY THOUGHTS TO GOD:

Taking up a cross is not appealing to me. It implies suffering and hardship. Yet You never ask me to do anything You have not been willing to do. May I grow in my faith to see beyond mere human point of view and have a God-view. I want to be Your follower. Please help me to turn from my selfish ways, take up my cross, and follow You. May I keep before me the truth that real benefit is not *gaining* the whole world, but *giving* up my life to You for joy, eternal life, and my rescued soul! You gave Your life for my soul. Nothing is more valuable. What a price you paid for me!

YOUR THOUGHTS TO GOD:

_____

_____

_____

_____

_____

_____

_____

_____

_____

_____

WHAT DO YOU WANT ME TO DO FOR YOU?

As Jesus approached Jericho, a blind beggar was sitting beside the road. When he heard the noise of a crowd going past, he asked what was happening. They told him that Jesus the Nazarene was going by. So he began shouting, "Jesus, Son of David, have mercy on me!"

"Be quiet!" the people in front yelled at him.

But he only shouted louder, "Son of David, have mercy on me!"

When Jesus heard him, he stopped and ordered that the man be brought to him. As the man came near, Jesus asked him, **"What do you want me to do for you?"**

"Lord," he said, "I want to see!"

And Jesus said, "All right, receive your sight! Your faith has healed you."

Instantly the man could see, and he followed Jesus, praising God. And all who saw it praised God, too.

LUKE 18:35–43 (NLT)

Have you ever thought about your answer to this question? This blind beggar confidently knew his answer and would not be silenced by anyone. His shouts to the Son of David for mercy stopped Jesus in his tracks. "What do you want me to do for you?" And the man knew exactly what he wanted Jesus to do for him.

The best part of this story is that Jesus did exactly what the blind man asked! Why? The blind beggar possessed *faith*. He knew what he wanted and *he asked for it*. Jesus responded, "Receive your sight!" and *instantly* the man could see.

What do you want Jesus to do for you? Do you have enough faith to ask?

MY THOUGHTS TO GOD:

Jesus, do I have faith to shout out to You and get your attention—no matter what the crowd says? Do I believe You are the One with the power to do what I ask? Do I *know* You can and will do it? Please, increase my faith in Your power.

YOUR THOUGHTS TO GOD:

_____

_____

_____

_____

_____

_____

_____

_____

_____

_____

WHERE CAN WE BUY BREAD TO FEED ALL THESE PEOPLE?

A huge crowd kept following him wherever he went, because they saw his miraculous signs as he healed the sick.

*Then Jesus climbed a hill and sat down with his disciples around him. (It was nearly time for the Jewish Passover celebration) Jesus soon saw a huge crowd of people coming to look for him. Turning to Philip, he asked, **"Where can we buy bread to feed all these people?"** He was testing Philip, for he already knew what he was going to do.*

Philip replied, "Even if we worked for months, we wouldn't have enough money to feed them!"

Then Andrew, Simon Peter's brother, spoke up. "There's a young boy here with five barley loaves and two fish. But what good is that with this huge crowd?"

"Tell everyone to sit down," Jesus said. So they all sat down on the grassy slopes. (The men alone numbered about 5,000.) Then Jesus took the loaves, gave thanks to God, and distributed them to the people. Afterward he did the same with the fish. And they all ate as much as they wanted.

After everyone was full, Jesus told his disciples, "Now gather the leftovers, so that nothing is wasted." So they picked up the pieces and filled twelve baskets with scraps left by the people who had eaten from the five barley loaves.

John 6:2–13 (NLT)
(See also Matthew 14, Mark 6, and Luke 9)

A little boy's lunch of five loaves of bread and two fish, 5,000 men fed and twelve basketfuls leftover. What a day! What a picnic! They had more (Far more!) leftover than what they started with. Can you imagine? I can't. Perhaps that's why I never tire of reading and hearing about this miracle.

How do we answer, "Where can we buy bread to feed all these people?" What can be done to address this problem? How can this be fixed?

I typically answer with obvious human reasoning: The problem is too big. It's impossible!

I can completely relate with Philip and Andrew's perspective. Money and food were scarce. Even if they had the money, there was no place to buy so much food on short notice. I just hear Philip's incredulous response, "You're asking *me*?!"

Have you faced an impossible situation and felt completely helpless and hopeless? You know that all you have in that moment isn't nearly enough. How tempting it is to give up and say, *This isn't going to work!*

Is Jesus seeking to stretch your faith? He already knows what He is going to do to solve the problems you face. He wants to bless you in unimaginable ways. But first, He wants you to trust Him.

How hard is it to trust Jesus, to have your faith stretched?

Wouldn't it be exciting to have more left over than what you started with?

MY THOUGHTS TO GOD:

Faith is power from You. Faith is confidence in You. Faith is ending with more than I started with—basketfuls of leftovers. My responsibility is bringing what I have and giving it all to You. Then You will perform the miracle and meet the need *far more abundantly than all that we ask or think* (Ephesians 3:20, ESV). Where can we buy bread to feed these people? As Ezekiel said, "Ah, Sovereign Lord, you alone know the answer to that!" (Ezekiel 37:3, NLT). I trust You to supply the answer.

YOUR THOUGHTS TO GOD:

_____

_____

_____

_____

_____

_____

_____

_____

_____

_____

WHO ARE YOU LOOKING FOR?

Early on Sunday morning, while it was still dark, Mary Magdalene came to the tomb and found that the stone had been rolled away from the entrance. She ran and found Simon Peter and the other disciple, the one whom Jesus loved. She said, "They have taken the Lord's body out of the tomb, and we don't know where they have put him!"

Peter and the other disciple started out for the tomb. They were both running, but the other disciple outran Peter and reached the tomb first. He stooped and looked in and saw the linen wrappings lying there, but he didn't go in. Then Simon Peter arrived and went inside. He also noticed the linen wrappings lying there, while the cloth that had covered Jesus' head was folded up and lying apart from the other wrappings. Then the disciple who had reached the tomb first also went in, and he saw and believed—for until then they still hadn't understood the Scriptures that said Jesus must rise from the dead. Then they went home.

Mary was standing outside the tomb crying, and as she wept, she stooped and looked in. She saw two white-robed angels, one sitting at the head and the other at the foot of the place where the body of Jesus had been lying. "Dear woman, why are you crying?" the angels asked her.

"Because they have taken away my Lord," she replied, "and I don't know where they have put him."

She turned to leave and saw someone standing there. It was Jesus, but she didn't recognize him. "Dear woman, why are you crying?" Jesus asked her. **"Who are you looking for?"**

She thought he was the gardener. "Sir," she said, "if you have taken him away, tell me where you have put him, and I will go and get him."

"Mary!" Jesus said.

She turned to him and cried out, "Rabboni!" (which is Hebrew for "Teacher").

"Don't cling to me," Jesus said, "for I haven't yet ascended to the Father. But go find my brothers and tell them, 'I am ascending to my Father and your Father, to my God and your God.'"

Mary Magdalene found the disciples and told them, "I have seen the Lord!" Then she gave them his message.

JOHN 20:1–18 (NLT)

Mary Magdalene, weeping and heart broken, went to the tomb to "care for Him." Believing what she had seen with her eyes, she knew the Master was dead.

Now not only was He dead but His body was gone. Several observations come to mind:

- ❖ She remained behind when the other two disciples, Peter and John, went back home.

- ❖ When she looked back into the tomb, she saw two angels. Unfazed, she answered their question and told them why she wept.

- ❖ She didn't recognize the Master until he spoke her name. Confirming what Jesus said earlier in John 10, "My sheep recognize my voice."

- ❖ When she recognized Him, her sorrow immediately disappeared, and joy and elation took over.

Jesus asks, *"Why are you weeping?"* and *"Who are you looking for?"* Why is your heart breaking, and "who" not *what* do you seek to mend it?

We look to many things and people for healing a broken heart when Jesus is the only One who can mend it.

Who are you looking for?

MY THOUGHTS TO GOD:

I pray I will recognize Your voice at all times, especially when my heart is broken. May my hope be strong in You even when I see contradicting evidence. Help me remember that heartache can be banished and turned to joy in a second when it is Your will. I need to keep before me that my life should always be about *You*—the One I am seeking. I must get that right!

YOUR THOUGHTS TO GOD:

_____

_____

_____

_____

_____

_____

_____

_____

_____

IF ALL YOU DO IS LOVE THE LOVABLE, DO YOU EXPECT A BONUS?

"You're familiar with the old written law, Love your friend, and its unwritten companion, Hate your enemy. I'm challenging that. I'm telling you to love your enemies. Let them bring out the best in you, not the worst. When someone gives you a hard time, respond with the energies of prayer, for then you are working out of your true selves, your God-created selves. This is what God does. He gives his best—the sun to warm and the rain to nourish—to everyone, regardless: the good and bad, the nice and nasty. **If all you do is love the lovable, do you expect a bonus?** Anybody can do that. If you simply say hello to those who greet you, do you expect a medal? Any run-of-the-mill sinner does that.

"In a word, what I'm saying is grow up. You're kingdom subjects. Now live like it. Live out your God-created identity. Live generously and graciously toward others, the way God lives toward you.

"Be especially careful when you are trying to be good so that you don't make a performance out of it. It might be good theater, but the God who made you won't be applauding.

"When you do something for someone else, don't call attention to yourself. You've seen them in action, I'm sure—play actors I call them—treating prayer meeting and street corner alike as a stage, acting compassionate as long as someone is watching, playing to the crowds. They get applause, true, but that's all they get. When you help someone out, don't think about how it looks. Just do it—quietly and unobtrusively. That is the way your God, who conceived you in love working behind the scenes, helps you out."

MATTHEW 5: 43–6:4 (THE MESSAGE)

I am struck with the words "do you expect?" Honestly, my answer would be yes. And obviously Jesus knows that! His response to my selfish expectations: "Grow up!" To do that, I must live out my God-created identity and start living generously and graciously toward others. Focusing on God's expectations rather than my own expectations will guide me to live as a Kingdom subject.

Loving the lovable is easy; loving your enemies isn't! Jesus tells us to allow our enemies to bring out the best in us, not the worst. This is a paradigm shift for me.

Why do we expect a medal or bonus from God for loving the lovable?

Why do we expect recognition and attention for doing only what is easy?

What needs to change in your thinking to let your enemies bring out the best in you?

MY THOUGHTS TO GOD:

May I be conscious of how much I expect. May I learn to live generously and follow Your example and love more—both the loving and the unloving. Help me to respond with the energies of prayer, giving my best from my God-created identity. I want to be gracious toward others because You are so gracious to me. Please change my focus from me to *You*, so I can do as You say: Grow up and live like a Kingdom subject.

YOUR THOUGHTS TO GOD:

_____

_____

_____

_____

_____

_____

_____

_____

_____

I HAVE DONE MANY GOOD WORKS. FOR WHICH ONE ARE YOU GOING TO STONE ME?

It was now winter, and Jesus was in Jerusalem at the time of Hanukkah, the Festival of Dedication. He was in the Temple, walking through the section known as Solomon's Colonnade. The people surrounded him and asked, "How long are you going to keep us in suspense? If you are the Messiah, tell us plainly."

Jesus replied, "I have already told you, and you don't believe me. The proof is the work I do in my Father's name. But you don't believe me because you are not my sheep. My sheep listen to my voice; I know them, and they follow me.

*Once again the people picked up stones to kill him. Jesus said, "At my Father's direction I have done many good works. **For which one are you going to stone me?**"*

They replied, "We're stoning you not for any good work, but for blasphemy! You, a mere man, claim to be God."

Jesus replied, "It is written in your own Scriptures that God said to certain leaders of the people, 'I say, you are gods!' (see Psalm 82:6) And you know that the Scriptures cannot be altered. So if those people who received God's message were called 'gods,' why do you call it blasphemy when I say, 'I am the Son of God'? After all, the Father set me apart and sent me into the world. Don't believe me unless I carry out my Father's work. But if I do his work, believe in the evidence of the miraculous works I have done, even if you don't believe me. Then you will know and understand that the Father is in me, and I am in the Father."

Once again they tried to arrest him, but he got away and left them. He went beyond the Jordan River near the place where John was first baptizing and stayed there awhile. And many followed him. "John didn't perform miraculous signs," they remarked to one another, "but everything he said about this man has come true." And many who were there believed in Jesus.

JOHN 10:22–27, 31–42 (NLT)

The things Jesus did backed up His statement, "I am the Son of God." The problem wasn't in lack of proof; they simply *would not believe* His claim.

His words led to two extreme, opposite reactions that day. One group reacted with anger and hatred. They wanted Him arrested and stoned to death. The other group followed Him and believed the evidence of His actions.

A *blasphemer* is a person who shows contempt or disrespect for God. The religious leaders hated Jesus, not because of the miracles and signs He performed, but for the words He spoke—His claim of deity. They disregarded Jesus' message and Lordship, and in so doing were guilty of blasphemy—the very crime they accused Him of committing.

Do we hate Him for being who He said He was—the Son of God? Or do we accept Him at His word and believe? The key to our actions and reactions is in believing, or not believing, that Jesus is who He claimed to be—the Christ and the Son of God.

MY THOUGHTS TO GOD:

I am startled at the hatred evidenced by not believing. Many times I struggle with believing. In those moments, the reactions I display do not offer proof that I am Your child. May I not dishonor You by throwing stones or yelling *Blasphemer*! May I take the evidence of Your actions that is right before my eyes and believe You are the Good Shepherd, and help me recognize Your voice.

YOUR THOUGHTS TO GOD:

_____

_____

_____

_____

_____

_____

_____

_____

_____

_____

WHO TOUCHED
MY ROBE?

Then a leader of the local synagogue, whose name was Jairus, arrived. When he saw Jesus, he fell at his feet, pleading fervently with him. "My little daughter is dying," he said. "Please come and lay your hands on her; heal her so she can live."

Jesus went with him, and all the people followed, crowding around him. A woman in the crowd had suffered for twelve years with constant bleeding. She had suffered a great deal from many doctors, and over the years she had spent everything she had to pay them, but she had gotten no better. In fact, she had gotten worse.

She had heard about Jesus, so she came up behind him through the crowd and touched his robe. For she thought to herself, "If I can just touch his robe, I will be healed." Immediately the bleeding stopped, and she could feel in her body that she had been healed of her terrible condition.

*Jesus realized at once that healing power had gone out from him, so he turned around in the crowd and asked, **"Who touched my robe?"***

His disciples said to him, "Look at this crowd pressing around you. How can you ask, 'Who touched me?'"

But he kept on looking around to see who had done it. Then the frightened woman, trembling at the realization of what had happened to her, came and fell to her knees in front of him and told him what she had done. And he said to her, "Daughter, your faith has made you well. Go in peace. Your suffering is over."

MARK 5:22-32 (NLT)

I love this story! So much is going on at once. The local synagogue leader came and asked Jesus to his home to heal his dying daughter. As always, a crowd surrounds Jesus. And within the crowd, a suffering woman prays for healing. She knows she doesn't even need to speak with Him. She is confident that touching His robe would be enough. And it was! After twelve years of illness, Jesus instantly healed this poor woman!

In that same moment, with the crowd pressing in on Him, Jesus feels healing power leave him. When He asked "Who touched my robe?" the disciples rebuff the question. The crowd was too thick—too many people were reaching out and touching Him to identify just one. But Jesus did. He *felt* the woman's faith.

Can you picture the scene? Trembling, the woman confessed on her knees that she was in desperate need of healing and had touched His robe. Imagine the comfort she must have felt when Jesus said, "your faith has made you well . . . your suffering is over."

Notice that He didn't say He made her well, but that her *faith* had ended her suffering. Do you have the kind of faith it takes to reach out and "touch" Jesus with complete confidence in His ability to heal you? Would He feel your faith?

MY THOUGHTS TO GOD:

After twelve years her suffering was over in a moment, all because of her faith. She had tried everything and nothing helped; she had only gotten worse. Help me remember that although many in the crowd touched You, only *she* had faith that You would meet her need and heal her. And You did! Immediately, You both knew what had happened. Her suffering was over. May I live each day with the faith to touch You and be healed.

YOUR THOUGHTS TO GOD:

_____

_____

_____

_____

_____

_____

_____

_____

_____

_____

WHY ARE YOU AFRAID?

When Jesus saw the crowd around him, he instructed his disciples to cross to the other side of the lake. Then one of the teachers of religious law said to him, "Teacher, I will follow you wherever you go."

But Jesus replied, "Foxes have dens to live in, and birds have nests, but the Son of Man has no place even to lay his head."

Another of his disciples said, "Lord, first let me return home and bury my father." But Jesus told him, "Follow me now. Let the spiritually dead bury their own dead."

Then Jesus got into the boat and started across the lake with his disciples. Suddenly, a fierce storm struck the lake, with waves breaking into the boat.

But Jesus was sleeping.

The disciples went and woke him up, shouting, "Lord, save us! We're going to drown!"

Jesus responded, "**Why are you afraid?** You have so little faith!"

Then he got up and rebuked the wind and waves, and suddenly there was a great calm.

The disciples were amazed. "Who is this man?" they asked. "Even the winds and waves obey him!"

MATTHEW 8:18–27 (NLT)

Why are you afraid?

Fear kills faith. The revelation of this truth should be life changing. And yet, we are still fearful.

Once I was on a fishing boat in Nova Scotia, Canada, miles from land, when a storm blew in. I felt so small (and seasick) lying there on the deck of that boat. The situation was entirely beyond my control. You can bet I felt afraid. So, I can completely relate with the disciples.

Many of these disciples were fishermen. I am certain they had experienced rough seas before. But the fierceness of this storm had them fearing for their lives. They shouted at the sleeping Lord Jesus, "Save us! We're going to drown."

The Lord, calm and in complete control, asked them, "Why are you afraid?" Without waiting for their response, He gave them the answer: "You have so little faith!"

When faced with my own storms I turn to II Timothy 1:7: *"For God gave us a spirit not of fear but of power and love and self-control."* (ESV)

What fears kill your faith? What is your antidote to fear?

MY THOUGHTS TO GOD:

I have come to You many times shouting, "Lord, save me. I'm going to drown." And You answer with complete confidence and authority, "Why are you so afraid? You have so little faith." Dear God, please help me to overcome my fears. Increase my faith. Do not let me forget that even the winds and the waves obey You—and so should I.

YOUR THOUGHTS TO GOD:

_____

_____

_____

_____

_____

_____

_____

_____

_____

_____

WHY ARE YOUR HEARTS FILLED WITH DOUBT?

Then the two from Emmaus told their story of how Jesus had appeared to them as they were walking along the road, and how they had recognized him as he was breaking the bread. And just as they were telling about it, Jesus himself was suddenly standing there among them. "Peace be with you," he said. But the whole group was startled and frightened, thinking they were seeing a ghost!

*"Why are you frightened?" he asked. "**Why are your hearts filled with doubt?** Look at my hands. Look at my feet. You can see that it's really me. Touch me and make sure that I am not a ghost, because ghosts don't have bodies, as you see that I do." As he spoke, he showed them his hands and his feet.*

Still they stood there in disbelief, filled with joy and wonder. Then he asked them, "Do you have anything here to eat?" They gave him a piece of broiled fish, and he ate it as they watched.

Then he said, "When I was with you before, I told you that everything written about me in the law of Moses and the prophets and in the Psalms must be fulfilled." Then he opened their minds to understand the Scriptures. And he said, "Yes, it was written long ago that the Messiah would suffer and die and rise from the dead on the third day. It was also written that this message would be proclaimed in the authority of his name to all the nations, beginning in Jerusalem: 'There is forgiveness of sins for all who repent.' You are witnesses of all these things.

LUKE 24:35-48 (NLT)

Have you ever had trouble believing what you see? Two followers of Jesus had walked from Jerusalem to Emmaus, seven miles. They talked intently about what had happened with Jesus. They pondered over the story the women related earlier that day—that the tomb was empty and Jesus was alive.

Jesus himself appeared and walked along with them. But they didn't recognize Him. When they arrived at their destination and asked Him to stay for dinner, they still didn't know it was Jesus who stood before them. In fact, it wasn't until He broke bread and gave thanks that they recognized Him. Then He disappeared.

The men were so excited to see Jesus that they decided to immediately return to Jerusalem so they could share the news with the others. My guess is their pace on the return trip was a little faster!

Back with the other disciples, they shared their story—they had seen Jesus! Surely their friends would have doubted them. It was too good to be true. And then, as if on cue, Jesus appeared amid the group.

Of course, the disciples were startled and frightened. They simply could not believe their eyes. To calm their fears, He reassured them: I am not a ghost. It's me, in a body with flesh and bones. Do you have something to eat?

He asked, "Why are your hearts filled with doubt?" All of what they had seen and experienced was to be expected; it had been prophesied since the beginning of time! Jesus patiently reminded them that everything written about Him in the law of Moses and the prophets had to be fulfilled. He explained that they were witnesses to that fulfillment. He opened their minds to understand the Scriptures and the promise, "There is forgiveness of sins for all who repent." That was the best part for them—and for us!

Is your heart filled with doubt? Read the Scriptures and ask Jesus to reveal His truth to you.

Do you believe Jesus suffered and died and rose from the dead on the third day? Have you repented and experienced forgiveness? What a privilege and joy to be a witness of these things! Now, how can you share your personal experience of meeting Jesus?

MY THOUGHTS TO GOD:

Please remove the doubts from my heart that I may believe. May I be filled with joy and wonder at Your magnificence and love. Open my mind to understand how the Scriptures were fulfilled so I can be a witness of these things.

Your thoughts to God:

_____

_____

_____

_____

_____

_____

_____

_____

_____

WHY DID YOU DOUBT ME?

Immediately after this, Jesus insisted that his disciples get back into the boat and cross to the other side of the lake, while he sent the people home. After sending them home, he went up into the hills by himself to pray. Night fell while he was there alone.

Meanwhile, the disciples were in trouble far away from land, for a strong wind had risen, and they were fighting heavy waves. About three o'clock in the morning Jesus came toward them, walking on the water. When the disciples saw him walking on the water, they were terrified. In their fear, they cried out, "It's a ghost!"

But Jesus spoke to them at once. "Don't be afraid," he said. "Take courage. I am here!"

Then Peter called to him, "Lord, if it's really you, tell me to come to you, walking on the water."

"Yes, come," Jesus said.

So Peter went over the side of the boat and walked on the water toward Jesus. But when he saw the strong wind and the waves, he was terrified and began to sink. "Save me, Lord!" he shouted.

*Jesus immediately reached out and grabbed him. "You have so little faith," Jesus said. **"Why did you doubt me?"***

When they climbed back into the boat, the wind stopped. Then the disciples worshiped him. "You really are the Son of God!" they exclaimed.

Matthew 14:22–32 (NLT)

Jesus had just heard the news about the beheading of John the Baptist. He had planned to go to a remote place to be alone and pray. But the crowds heard where he was going and when he arrived by boat, they were waiting for him. So, he changed his plans. He healed the sick and met their needs—including feeding all of them with a young boy's donation of five loaves of bread and two fish.

After a long, emotionally exhausting day, He sent the disciples back across the lake so He could be alone and pray.

Meanwhile the disciples fought a storm and heavy waves. In the midst of this dark and troubled hour, they saw a ghost walking on the water!

I would be terrified, wouldn't you?

But Jesus spoke: "Don't be afraid. Take courage. I am here!"

Peter, in faith, climbed over the side of the boat and began to walk on the water toward Jesus. But then fear took over. Peter started to sink into the dark, churning waves. and cried out, "Save me, Lord!" And He did.

Why do you have so little faith? Jesus asked Peter.

It's the same question He asks us today. *Why do you doubt me?*

What causes doubt in your life? Could it be lack of faith, lack of worship, unbelief, fear?

MY THOUGHTS TO GOD:

I doubt because I have so little faith and too much fear. Just like You said to Peter. You are the Son of God. If I would remember that, my faith would grow larger than my fears. May I keep Your words in my heart, "Don't be afraid. Take courage. I am here!" When I am in trouble, in the storm and fighting the waves, Jesus please say to me, "Yes, come."

YOUR THOUGHTS TO GOD:

_____

_____

_____

_____

_____

_____

_____

_____

WHY DO YOU HAVE SUCH EVIL THOUGHTS IN YOUR HEARTS?

Jesus climbed into a boat and went back across the lake to his own town. Some people brought to him a paralyzed man on a mat.

Seeing their faith, Jesus said to the paralyzed man, "Be encouraged, my child! Your sins are forgiven."

But some of the teachers of religious law said to themselves, "That's blasphemy! Does he think he's God?"

*Jesus knew what they were thinking, so he asked them, "**Why do you have such evil thoughts in your hearts?** Is it easier to say 'Your sins are forgiven,' or 'Stand up and walk'?"*

So I will prove to you that the Son of Man has the authority on earth to forgive sins. Then Jesus turned to the paralyzed man and said, "Stand up, pick up your mat, and go home!" And the man jumped up and went home!

Fear swept through the crowd as they saw this happen. And they praised God for sending a man with such great authority.

MATTHEW 9:1–8 (NLT)

The religious teachers did not like authority. What a surprise! Do you like authority?

I struggle with this lesson of submission; I believe most people do. We start exerting our self-will at an early age—remember your child's "terrible twos"?

In this scene, Jesus lays out our options. We can either:

- Willingly submit to God's authority, or
- Fight against His authority and foster evil thoughts in our hearts.

To prove His sovereignty and power on earth to forgive sins, Jesus told the paralyzed man to get up and go home—forgiven and healed!

Look at the contrast of the crowd's two reactions:

Some people praised God. The paralyzed man was healed—and excited! His friends and those who understood Jesus' power were grateful to God for sending a man with such great authority. They *knew* Jesus indeed had the power to heal and forgive.

Others, specifically the religious teachers, hated Jesus. Animosity consumed them. They *hated* His authority. "That's blasphemy! Does he think he's God?" No awe, no excitement, no gratefulness, only hatred and resentment filled their hearts.

How do you view authority, specifically God's authority?

How do you limit God's power in your life by not submitting to His authority?

Do you see a connection between despising authority and evil thoughts?

MY THOUGHTS TO GOD:

How do I view Your authority, God? Do I willingly submit and allow Your power to manifest in my life? I want to say I do, but You know I balk too often. Like an ungrateful child my heart yells, "You can't tell me what to do."

May I remember from past experiences that despising Your authority fills my heart with anger, hatred, resentment, and bitterness. I ask for faith and complete confidence in Your authority and healing power. May I strive to live the prayer, "Thy kingdom come, Thy will be done on earth as it is in heaven."

YOUR THOUGHTS TO GOD:

_____

_____

_____

_____

_____

_____

_____

_____

_____

WHY DO YOU HAVE SO LITTLE FAITH?

"Look at the lilies and how they grow. They don't work or make their clothing, yet Solomon in all his glory was not dressed as beautifully as they are. And if God cares so wonderfully for flowers that are here today and thrown into the fire tomorrow, he will certainly care for you. **Why do you have so little faith?**

"And don't be concerned about what to eat and what to drink. Don't worry about such things. These things dominate the thoughts of unbelievers all over the world, but your Father already knows your needs. Seek the Kingdom of God above all else, and he will give you everything you need.

"So don't be afraid, little flock. For it gives your Father great happiness to give you the Kingdom.

"Sell your possessions and give to those in need. This will store up treasure for you in heaven! And the purses of heaven never get old or develop holes. Your treasure will be safe; no thief can steal it and no moth can destroy it. Wherever your treasure is, there the desires of your heart will also be."

LUKE 12: 27-34 (NLT)

Worry is a constant struggle. *Why do we have so little faith?*

Every time I think I am making progress in my battle against worry, something comes along and forces me to question where my treasure and trust really lie.

In verse 21 of this same chapter Jesus said, "Yes, a person is a fool to store up earthly wealth but not have a rich relationship with God." There is no sin in having wealth. But it *is* sinful to seek wealth at the expense of developing a rich relationship with God.

For me, worry, particularly when it comes to having my physical needs met, is a matter of fear and trust. Do I believe the Father truly desires to give me the Kingdom? Do I believe the Father already knows my needs? Am I seeking the Kingdom of God above all else? Do I *know* He will give me everything I need?

Seeking security is natural, but if we look to our belongings or wealth to comfort us, we will never have enough. Perhaps that's why Jesus encouraged His followers to sell their possessions and give to the poor. By helping to meet others' needs we can increase our faith as we rely on God to meet ours.

Every time the daffodils bloom in early spring, their beauty reminds me how much more valuable I am to God than the flowers. So are you.

Do you give generously to those in need—or do you hold back for security's sake?

Do you believe the Father knows and will supply your needs?

Why do you have so little faith?

MY THOUGHTS TO GOD:

I hear You asking me this question daily! Do I receive Your gift of the Kingdom and give You great happiness? May my thoughts be dominated not with worry about my needs but with seeking Your Kingdom. Help me to see and give to those in need. Storing treasure in Your care and changing my heart's desire is the way to make You happy.

YOUR THOUGHTS TO GOD:

_____

_____

_____

_____

_____

_____

_____

_____

_____

And why do you, by your traditions, violate the direct commandments of God?

Some Pharisees and teachers of religious law now arrived from Jerusalem to see Jesus. They asked him, "Why do your disciples disobey our age-old tradition? For they ignore our tradition of ceremonial hand washing before they eat."

*Jesus replied, "**And why do you, by your traditions, violate the direct commandments of God?** For instance, God says, 'Honor your father and mother,' and 'Anyone who speaks disrespectfully of father or mother must be put to death.' But you say it is all right for people to say to their parents, 'Sorry, I can't help you. For I have vowed to give to God what I would have given to you.' In this way, you say they don't need to honor their parents. And so you cancel the word of God for the sake of your own tradition. You hypocrites! Isaiah was right when he prophesied about you, for he wrote,*

'These people honor me with their lips, but their hearts are far from me.

Their worship is a farce, for they teach man-made ideas as commands from God.'"

MATTHEW 15:1–9 (NLT)

Do our traditions violate the commandments of God?

The religious leaders complained that Jesus' disciples did not wash their hands properly before eating. The washing wasn't about germs, but about ceremony and tradition. I know it seems ridiculous, but do we cling to ridiculous traditions as well?

Jesus chose not to join in the hand-washing debate. Instead, He pointed out a commandment both His disciples and the religious leaders certainly knew. Commandment number five of the Ten Commandments (Exodus 20:1–17): *"Honor your father and mother. Then you will live a long, full life in the land the Lord your God is giving you"* (NLT).

He followed up by quoting Isaiah 29:13, another passage that would have been very familiar to the religious leaders: "They teach man-made ideas as commands from God."

Teaching man-made ideas as commands from God. BAM! *That* was the heart of their problem! *That* is, religion. Tradition, religion, teaching man-made ideas as commands from God—those things are still problems for people today.

The religious leaders knew and taught the Scriptures. Because they seemed to *intentionally* miss the point of God's Law, Jesus called them on their hypocrisy.

They followed the philosophy of "do as I say, NOT as I do." Do we do the same? Do our actions scream *Rebellion!* and in so doing kill the cause of Christ?

Do you cancel the word of God for the sake of your own tradition?

How would you define a hypocrite?

MY THOUGHTS TO GOD:

I pray my heart will not be far from You and my worship a farce! Are my traditions more important to me than Your commandments? While I despise hypocrites, am I one? No matter what I show on the outside, it's what is on the inside—my heart—that starves or feeds the hypocrite. May I focus on my heart and not hand-washing.

In Matthew 22:37–40 (NLT), Jesus replied, "'You must love the Lord your God with all your heart, all your soul, and all your mind. This is the first and greatest commandment. A second is equally important: 'Love your neighbor as yourself.' The entire law and all the demands of the prophets are based on these two commandments."

YOUR THOUGHTS TO GOD:

_____

_____

_____

_____

_____

_____

_____

_____

WHY DO YOU SEEK TO KILL ME?

About the middle of the feast Jesus went up into the temple and began teaching. The Jews therefore marveled, saying, "How is it that this man has learning, when he has never studied?"

So Jesus answered them, "My teaching is not mine, but his who sent me. If anyone's will is to do God's will, he will know whether the teaching is from God or whether I am speaking on my own authority. The one who speaks on his own authority seeks his own glory; but the one who seeks the glory of him who sent him is true, and in him there is no falsehood. Has not Moses given you the law? Yet none of you keeps the law. **Why do you seek to kill me?***"*

The crowd answered, "You have a demon! Who is seeking to kill you?"

Jesus answered them, "I did one work, and you all marvel at it. Moses gave you circumcision (not that it is from Moses, but from the fathers), and you circumcise a man on the Sabbath. If on the Sabbath a man receives circumcision, so that the law of Moses may not be broken, are you angry with me because on the Sabbath I made a man's whole body well? (See John 5:1–18) Do not judge by appearances, but judge with right judgment."

Some of the people of Jerusalem therefore said, "Is not this the man whom they seek to kill? And here he is, speaking openly, and they say nothing to him! Can it be that the authorities really know that this is the Christ? But we know where this man comes from, and when the Christ appears, no one will know where he comes from."

So Jesus proclaimed, as he taught in the temple, "You know me, and you know where I come from. But I have not come of my own accord. He who sent me is true, and him you do not know. I know him, for I come from him, and he sent me."

So they were seeking to arrest him, but no one laid a hand on him, because his hour had not yet come. Yet many of the people believed in him. They said, "When the Christ appears, will he do more signs than this man has done?"

JOHN 7:14–31 (ESV)

The people in the crowd based their perspectives on what they *thought* they knew about Jesus: He was a carpenter from the area with no formal education or training—He had no right to any authority. He *couldn't* be the Messiah because they "knew" where he was from.

In THE MESSAGE, verse 24 reads, *"Don't be nitpickers; use your head—and heart!—to discern what is right, to test what is authentically right."* Are you a nitpicker? Do you use your head and heart to discern what is right? Do you make things up to make yourself look good? Or, do you stick to the facts? What are the facts? How do you tamper with reality and why?

MY THOUGHTS TO GOD:

This is a tough one! I realize they wanted to kill You, not for doing good, but for being good—shining a light in the darkness. I know this was a battle for authority! May I seek to honor You, and not seek to kill. Will the crowd be split because of my belief in You? May I not just *think* I know You! Let me search You out and discern what is right.

YOUR THOUGHTS TO GOD:

_____

_____

_____

_____

_____

_____

_____

_____

_____

But if I'm telling the truth, why don't you believe me?

Jesus once again addressed them: "I am the world's Light. No one who follows me stumbles around in the darkness. I provide plenty of light to live in."

The Pharisees objected, "All we have is your word on this. We need more than this to go on."

Jesus replied, "You're right that you only have my word. But you can depend on it being true. I know where I've come from and where I go next. You don't know where I'm from or where I'm headed. You decide according to what you can see and touch. I don't make judgments like that." . . .

Jesus said, "You're tied down to the mundane; I'm in touch with what is beyond your horizons. You live in terms of what you see and touch. I'm living on other terms. I told you that you were missing God in all this. You're at a dead end. If you won't believe I am who I say I am, you're at the dead end of sins. You're missing God in your lives."

Then Jesus turned to the Jews who had claimed to believe in him. "If you stick with this, living out what I tell you, you

are my disciples for sure. Then you will experience for your-
selves the truth, and the truth will free you."

Surprised, they said, "But we're descendants of Abraham.
We've never been slaves to anyone. How can you say, "The
truth will free you?'

Jesus said, "I tell you most solemnly that anyone who chooses
a life of sin is trapped in a dead-end life and is, in fact, a
slave . . .

"Why can't you understand one word I say? Here's why:
You can't handle it. You're from your father, the Devil, and
all you want to do is please him. He was a killer from the
very start. He couldn't stand the truth because there wasn't
a shred of truth in him . . . Can any one of you convict me
of a single misleading word, a single sinful act? **But if I'm**
telling the truth, why don't you believe me? *Anyone on*
God's side listens to God's words. This is why you're not lis-
tening—because you're not on God's side."

JOHN 8:12–15, 23–24, 31–34, 43–47 (THE MESSAGE)

I t is the same for us today. Jesus asks, "Why don't you believe me?" And we respond like the Pharisees did: We need more than Your word to go on.

We are tied down to the mundane and forget that God sees beyond our horizons. We want to live on our terms and trust only what we can *see* and *touch*.

Are you at a dead-end? Do you need more than God's Word to go on in your life?

Jesus tells us He is the Truth and the Light. He offers freedom.

Truth vs. Lie
Free vs. Slave
Light vs. Darkness

If you choose not to trust Him, what is your hope?

MY THOUGHTS TO GOD:

You have given me hope. Your truth sets me free! Please help me realize how much I depend on seeing and touching when all I need is to trust You. Don't allow me to remain tied down by the mundane. May I believe Your word, be on Your side, and see what You see beyond my horizons. I know You are telling the truth, and I believe You!

YOUR THOUGHTS TO GOD:

_____

_____

_____

_____

_____

_____

_____

_____

PLEASE GIVE
ME A DRINK?

So he left Judea and returned to Galilee. He had to go through Samaria on the way. Eventually he came to the Samaritan village of Sychar, near the field that Jacob gave to his son Joseph. Jacob's well was there; and Jesus, tired from the long walk, sat wearily beside the well about noontime.

*Soon a Samaritan woman came to draw water, and Jesus said to her, **"Please give me a drink."** He was alone at the time because his disciples had gone into the village to buy some food.*

The woman was surprised, for Jews refuse to have anything to do with Samaritans. She said to Jesus, "You are a Jew, and I am a Samaritan woman. Why are you asking me for a drink?"

Jesus replied, "If you only knew the gift God has for you and who you are speaking to, you would ask me, and I would give you living water."

"But sir, you don't have a rope or a bucket," she said, "and this well is very deep. Where would you get this living water?

And besides, do you think you're greater than our ancestor Jacob, who gave us this well? How can you offer better water than he and his sons and his animals enjoyed?"

Jesus replied, "Anyone who drinks this water will soon become thirsty again. But those who drink the water I give will never be thirsty again. It becomes a fresh, bubbling spring within them, giving them eternal life."

"Please, sir," the woman said, "give me this water! Then I'll never be thirsty again, and I won't have to come here to get water."

"Go and get your husband," Jesus told her.

"I don't have a husband," the woman replied.

Jesus said, "You're right! You don't have a husband—for you have had five husbands, and you aren't even married to the man you're living with now. You certainly spoke the truth!"

"Sir," the woman said, "you must be a prophet. So tell me, why is it that you Jews insist that Jerusalem is the only place of worship, while we Samaritans claim it is here at Mount Gerizim, where our ancestors worshiped?"

Jesus replied, "Believe me, dear woman, the time is coming when it will no longer matter whether you worship the Father on this mountain or in Jerusalem. You Samaritans know very little about the one you worship, while we Jews know all about him, for salvation comes through the Jews. But the time is coming—indeed it's here now—when true worshipers will worship the Father in spirit and in truth. The Father is looking for those who will worship him that way. For God is Spirit, so those who worship him must worship in spirit and in truth."

The woman said, "I know the Messiah is coming—the one who is called Christ. When he comes, he will explain everything to us."

Then Jesus told her, "I Am the Messiah!"

JOHN 4:3–26 (NLT)

I *love* this story!

First, the Scripture states "He had to go through Samaria." Why? Do you think it was to speak to this woman at the well?

The woman was shocked that Jesus asked her for a drink of water. She questioned Him because the Jews had a long history of dislike for the Samaritans.

Then, He told her she *needed* the Living Water!

Confused, she pointed out that He didn't even have a way to draw water. How, then, could He offer any water—much less "Living Water?"

Patiently, Jesus explained that His water will become a spring of water welling up to eternal life. If she drinks from it, she will never be thirsty again.

Never thirst again? She wanted that!

Then Jesus threw her a curve ball: "Go, call your husband and come back."

"I don't have one," she replied. She spoke honestly. Her need—her thirst—was evident. And Jesus was the only One who could help.

Finally, He told her directly, plainly—"I am the Messiah."

Because this woman believed, many in her town came to know Jesus. I think that's why He had to go through Samaria.

He found the woman at the well and asked for help—when He knew all along she was the one in need.

How will you answer His request? Will you give Him a drink? Will you let Him meet your needs?

MY THOUGHTS TO GOD:

Oh Lord, this woman at the well had great needs and longing in her heart. You found her just as You found me. You ask for a drink, but I am the one with the need that only You can meet. May I seek to know where You are working and ask to join, accepting the living water You offer and worship You in the Spirit and in truth.

YOUR THOUGHTS TO GOD:

_____

_____

_____

_____

_____

_____

_____

_____

DO YOU HAVE ANY IDEA HOW DIFFICULT IT IS FOR THE RICH TO ENTER GOD'S KINGDOM?

Another day, a man stopped Jesus and asked, "Teacher, what good thing must I do to get eternal life?"

Jesus said, "Why do you question me about what's good? God is the One who is good. If you want to enter the life of God, just do what he tells you."

The man asked, "What in particular?"

Jesus said, "Don't murder, don't commit adultery, don't steal, don't lie, honor your father and mother, and love your neighbor as you do yourself."

The young man said, "I've done all that. What's left?"

"If you want to give it all you've got," Jesus replied, "go sell your possessions; give everything to the poor. All your wealth will then be in heaven. Then come follow me."

That was the last thing the young man expected to hear. And so, crestfallen, he walked away. He was holding on tight to a lot of things, and he couldn't bear to let go.

*As he watched him go, Jesus told his disciples, "**Do you have any idea how difficult it is for the rich to enter God's kingdom?** Let me tell you, it's easier to gallop a camel through a needle's eye than for the rich to enter God's kingdom."*

The disciples were staggered. "Then who has any chance at all?"

Jesus looked hard at them and said, "No chance at all if you think you can pull it off yourself. Every chance in the world if you trust God to do it."

MATTHEW 19:16–26 (THE MESSAGE)

This man knew something was missing in his life. What was it? He asked Jesus and was delighted to hear the checklist of do's and don'ts. *Ah, this is good! All this I've done.* Still, something was missing. But, what?

Can you imagine the thoughts that must have run through his head when Jesus told him to sell everything and follow Him? *You are kidding, right? You want me to store wealth in heaven, let go of my earthly security, give to the poor, and follow you?*

The Bible doesn't share his thoughts. We only know that "Crestfallen, he walked away." Heartbroken, he gave up.

Have you walked away from a God-opportunity or God-invitation because you couldn't bear to let go of some*thing*?

"Hold everything in your hands lightly. Otherwise it hurts when God pries your fingers open."

CORRIE TEN BOOM

MY THOUGHTS TO GOD:

You know my heart and know this lesson is a tough one for me, just as it was for the disciples. Keeping a list of do's and don'ts will never fill the void. I cannot enter the life of God on my own. May I seek every opportunity to trust You. I know I have no chance if I try to do it on my own. Please help me hold "things" lightly, not tightly, and to be able to let go when You ask it of me.

YOUR THOUGHTS TO GOD:

_____

_____

_____

_____

_____

_____

_____

_____

_____

ARE YOU READY TO ROUGH IT?

On the road someone asked if he could go along. "I'll go with you, wherever," he said.

Jesus was curt: "**Are you ready to rough it?** We're not staying in the best inns, you know."

Jesus said to another, "Follow me."

He said, "Certainly, but first excuse me for a couple of days, please, I have to make arrangements for my father's funeral."

Jesus refused. "First things first. Your business is life, not death. And life is urgent: Announce God's kingdom!"

Then another said, "I'm ready to follow you, Master, but first excuse me while I get things straightened out at home."

Jesus said, "No procrastination. No backward looks. You can't put God's kingdom off till tomorrow. Seize the day."

LUKE 9:57–62 (THE MESSAGE)

I n summary, I am compelled to add this one last question. I know it makes thirty-two questions, but there is no extra charge for this one! And I am only sharing thoughts. Of course, I welcome your thoughts as well!

As you have read through the scripture passages and answered these questions, it is my prayer that you and I would be willing and able to answer YES to this closing question.

Earlier in this chapter Jesus

- Sent out the Twelve and gave them authority and power
- Fed 5,000-plus with only five loaves and a couple of fish
- Asked the disciples, "Who am I?"
- Climbed a mountain to pray with Peter, James and John, who saw Jesus in His glory with Moses and Elijah
- Healed a man's only son when the disciples could not
- Told the disciples that he was about to be betrayed
- Settled an argument among the disciples over who would be the greatest
- Reminded James and John *not* to incinerate the Samaritans for their unwillingness to extend hospitality

Now He asks, "Are you ready to rough it?"

The events listed in this chapter attest to what it means to follow Him. I find it interesting (and convicting) that both people in this passage who wanted to follow Him said,

"But first excuse me . . ." Have you ever told God, "I will, but first . . ."? I know I have. *But first let me . . .*

- *finish school*
- *marry*
- *raise my children*
- *make money*
- *have a career*
- *have some fun, have time for myself*

What if He does "let me"? Have I or will I miss God's opportunities?

Jesus said, "Your business is life . . . life is urgent . . . announce God's kingdom! . . . No procrastination; No backward looks; you can't put God's kingdom off till tomorrow. Seize the day."

May we focus our lives on God's will and unique plan for each one of us and *seize* the day!

ABOUT THE AUTHOR

 RISA BAKER is the wife of her life-long friend, Dan. She and her husband met when they were five and remain best friends! She is mother and mother-in-law to five, and grandmother to four. Business owner, life coach and author are additional "hats."

She is passionate about encouraging others to discover meaning and mission in their lives to mobilize and impact the world for God. Her life's purpose provides the opportunity to speak and train nationally and internationally. She also serves on the board of directors for two non-profit organizations.

You may contact Risa at risa@risabaker.com

CPSIA information can be obtained at www.ICGtesting.com
Printed in the USA
LVOW12s1140251113

362737LV00003B/122/P